Quartered Enlightenment

Culture Saisonnière

Poems by

Trisha Georgiou

Pool boy Publishing

Moline, Illinois

Quartered Enlightenment

Poetry
By Trisha Georgiou

Copyright © Trisha Georgiou 2013
Pages 106

Published by:
Pool boy Publishing
P.O. Box 721
Moline, Illinois
www.PoolboyPublishing.com

Cover Design by Brandt Design Team

Printed in the United States of America

ISBN 978-098870594-4

All Rights Reserved.
This book contains material protected under International and Federal Copyright Treaties. With the exception of brief quotations for the sole purpose of reviews or comparative articles, no part of this book may be reproduced in any manner without prior written permission from the Author and/ or Publisher.

Dedication

To all lovers, readers, writers of poetry, and
to my three cherished spirits of enlightenment,
may this book lead, guide, and inspire you to
go places not yet discovered.

Acknowledgements

First and foremost, an eternal and loud THANK YOU is extended to my publisher and my dear friend David L. Cahoon. Without his brilliance on and off the page, Quartered Enlightenment would not exist. Thank you for every moment, every text, every comma, and every glass of wine. What you have given me can only be felt, not expressed.

A further heartfelt thank you is also extended most appreciatively to:

Nathalie Markovits, my dear cousin who guided with her amazing gifts and patience editing the French translations. It meant the world to me to work on this project with you.

Poet Sandra Marchetti, for writing
A Fruitful Return: Reflections on Quartered Enlightenment.
I am forever thankful our garden and poetry paths crossed.

Lori Perkins, Total Printing Systems, I can not thank you enough. Your dedication to the written word is unsurpassed.

Brandt/Doubleday design team for your creative design genius for the cover.

Elsa for assistance with proofreading and formatting, Finley for creativity and spreading joy, and Zane for your skills fixing all of my computer issues and website design. Thank you for being my children and supporting me through this entire process.

Marcus Christensen, Pool boy Publishing technical specialist, thank you for managing the long lists of to- dos.
Your brilliance is appreciated.

Dewey's Copper Café, Moline, Ill., to Salma, Esra, Kelsey, April, and Ed, who kept the blackberry sage tea brewing and my favourite writing spot warm.

And finally, to The Midwest Writing Center, you are my writing family. Thank you for years of support, encouragement, and a place to call home.

Table of Contents

Foreword written by David L. Cahoon
Preface
I. Summer
    Alone in Silence..............................15
    The Beginning................................17
    Sharing the Shadow of the Moon......19
    As Heat Rises.................................23
    Summer Solstice.............................25
    Summer Wedding...........................29

II. Autumn
    Cool Breezes of Consciousness........33
    Oppressive Heat..............................37
    Autumn Equinox.............................39
    The Garden Gate............................41
    Autumn..47

III. Winter
    Death in Living..............................50
    She Who Questions Life..................61
    Waiting in Winter...........................63
    Winter Solstice..............................65
    Lenten Journey..............................67
    Waiting on Spring..........................71

IV. Spring
    The Melting of Snow...............75
    Rebirth....................................77
    May Day.................................81
    The Gate Turns Warm..............85
    Transformation........................88
    Reflections..............................95

A Fruitful Return: Reflections on Quartered Enlightenment
by Poet Sandra Marchetti

Pages for Reflection

About the Author

Foreword

What you're about to read transcends the idea of a traditional poetry collection. Though each poem is powerful enough to stand on its own as a complete thought, a complete story, Quartered Enlightenment is something more of a novel than it is a book that may colloquially be defined in the genre, poetry. This story of the evolution of innocence is told through the license granted by rhyme and rhythm, with a strong voice and meter that only poetry can utilize. By using this writing method, the interpretative visions are opened greater than traditional writing allows.

As a collaborator in this process, in order to convey the many messages being expressed, I witnessed an author who expanded her creativity through cultivating her imagination. Though, through this cultivation, and ultimately the visual diagramming of the story, what once was a collection of garden poems blossomed into a story that is emotionally wrenching by anyone who has loved, or has sought the help from a divine hand.

Having been an entrepreneur since my earliest memory, it is rewarding for me to take the intangible and make it tangible. Turning a brainstorming result into a "thing" that others can feel and experience is satisfying. In the pages that follow, there is a palpable experience that has been removed from the realm of conceptual, and is now rooted deeply in the fertile soil of your own personal experience.

It has been by great serendipitous honor to be connected with this, what I call, poetic novella. Just as time relentlessly brings forth the life experience, the time that elapsed while editing this book has brought me closer to seeing how the unexpected can bring great, before unquantifiable and unfathomable, returns.

After finishing Quartered Enlightenment, close your eyes, take a few breaths, and collect the images and emotions in your mind. Grant yourself a meditative connection with the seasons that have just erupted around you, and if our message was successful, inside of you. Then, write these reflections on the blank pages in the back. Don't worry about your punctuation or grammar. Just let the ink flow!

I bet you'll feel better about something. Just as Trish and I have done, write what you feel, then learn from, and live by, your words.

David L. Cahoon
Pool boy Publishing
Exotic Imports

A Word Before...

Quartered Enlightenment is an illuminating tale of love and spiritual discovery told in English, complemented by French, then compressed into a single book of poetry.

The aesthetic qualities of language utilized throughout this work are specific to this literary genus. Each poem has its own unique meaning and purpose.

However, by reading the poems in sequential order, the specific characteristics of the story arc are revealed. As the protagonist moves through each season of her life, she discovers the many meanings, and uncountable layers, of love.

French translations are featured on the left hand side of the opened pages, which correspond to the original English poems on the right hand side.

It is my hope and intent by including the French translations, an enhanced level of artistic and linguistic beauty will provide a deeper perspective into the story. While experiencing this romantic language, the translations also remind us how we are all connected as humans, though speaking in different tongues, and living in different lands.

We are intertwined; appreciating art, interpreting poetry, gardening, self-discovery, and most importantly, with love.

With deepest gratitude,
Trisha Georgiou

Summer

When the tremulous radius of a summer night
fills with twinkling stars and the moon itself
is full. I am slowly drawn into a state of
enhanced sensitivity made of friendship and
disdain for the world and eternity.

~ Immanuel Kant

Seule dans le Silence

Pages tissées parfaitement ensembles. Plantes fleuries colorées et vertes. Elles m'accueillent après ma dévotion religieuse, dans l'attente de m'accompagner.

Le soleil brille formant de la rosée sur mon verre de thé glacé sucré, des traces de menthe fraîche et de framboises juste récoltées flottent à quelques mètres.

Aux confins sûrs de mon jardin je peux voyager à travers le monde. Je me perds dans les terres étrangères juste en tournant la page.

Sur la véranda un après-midi entier s'écoule, le même Dimanche au fils des ans, entourée de livres et de plantes, seule dans le silence.

La fin d'après-midi jette des ombres sur le jardin. Les mots, la fin, seulement lire. Je me lève de mon sanctuaire paisible avec une pensée soudaine de courage.

Mon écharpe et mon sac à la main, je quitte le calme de mon jardin, avec le besoin d'explorer le monde et de trouver mon histoire inédite.

Alone in Silence

Pages woven perfectly together.
Plants blooming colourful and green.
They welcome me returning from worship,
waiting to accompany me.

The sun shines brightly creating dew on my glass
from melting ice in sweetened tea,
with hints of fresh mint and raspberries
harvested only a few feet away.

In the safe confines of my garden
I can travel the world.
I lose myself in foreign lands
by only turning the page.

On the veranda an entire afternoon spent,
the same over the years of passing Sundays,
surrounded by books and plants,
alone in silence.

Late afternoon cast shadows on the garden.
The words, the end, just read.
I rise from my place of security and peace
with an emerging thought of courage.

My scarf and my bag in hand
I leave the quiet of my garden,
with the need to explore the world
and find an unpublished story.

The Beginning

Sans le savoir, je suis tombé dans son monde. Était-ce par chance ou par hasard? Était-ce une poussée prédéterminée par le cosmos ou une main angélique qui nous amène à rencontrer?

Dans le premier coup d'oeil à nos yeux se rencontrèrent. Son âme a la mienne en me permettant de voir son esprit se rendre la paix.

Un sourire gracieux échangé des salutations. Son énergie calmer. Sa voix invitant conversation intéressante, une ouverture pour les êtres conscients.

Dans son espace, ce nouveau monde découvert, le temps et ma vie a changé pour toujours. Était transformé sa vie comme la mienne quand je suis tombé dans son aura? Sa présence planté connexion

invitant de nouveaux échanges pour les graines tombèrent sur mon cœur de plus en plus cette *fondation.*

The Beginning

Unknowingly, I stumbled into his world.
Was it by chance or by fate?
Was it a predetermined push by the cosmos,
or an angelic hand leading us to meet?

Within the first glance our eyes met.
His soul drew mine in
allowing me to see his spirit,
surrendering peace.

A gracious smile exchanging greetings.
His energy calming. His voice inviting
interesting conversation,
an opening for mindful beings.

In his space, this new discovered world,
time and my life forever altered.
Was his life as transformed as mine
when I stumbled into his aura?

His presence planted connection
inviting further exchange
for the seeds fell unto my heart
growing this foundation.

Partage de l'ombre de la Lune

J'ai frappé à sa porteavec joncs de inconnu émotion.Répondit-il. Son sourire m'a invité.Dans ce seuil, une étreinte chaleureuse fondre le fardeau de la journée, les craintes de ce soir.

Son charme m'a conduit plus loin,en soulevant le poids de mes épaules, enprenant mon sac et le sac d'offres nouvelles.Il a remplacé la lourdeur des un verre de chardonnay,tout en exprimant un intérêt dans ma journée.

Sa belle table, fixé pour la royauté.Linge de maison, des plats, des hors-d'œuvre, et l'ambiance, parfait. Son attention aux détails avec chacun de mes souhaitez voir. conversation, le partage des idées, des rires.trouver du réconfort dans la connexion à un autre être.

Permettre d'être conduite, guidé à de nouvelles choses, précieux.Mais exposure mon moi authentique à une autre âme, étrangère.Par sentant son acceptation, de l'amitié, et la grâce,le dernier bit de la peur, l'insécurité décoloration,mon mur de pierre de protection, en train d'imploser.

Sharing the Shadow of the Moon

I knocked on his door
With rushes of emotions unknown.
He answered. His smile invited me.
In the threshold, a warm embrace
melting away the day's burdens, tonight's fears.

His charm led me further,
by lifting the weight from my shoulders,
taking my purse and the bag of fresh offerings.
He replaced the heaviness with a glass of chardonnay
while expressing interest in my day.

His table beautiful, set for royalty.
Linens, dishes, hors d'oeuvres, and ambiance, *perfect.*
His attention to detail with my every wish seen.
Sharing conversation, ideas, laughter.
Finding comfort in connecting to another being.

Allowing to be led, guided to new things, precious.
But exposing my authentic self to another soul, foreign.
By feeling his acceptance, friendship, and grace,
the last bit of fear, insecurity fading
my stone wall of protection, imploding.

Malgré lingerings intemporels, le jour est tombé à la nuit.Réalité arrive maintenant à ma conscience. Nous sommes retournés au seuil de cette époque transformé.je suis entré dans son monde comme un ami, mais parce que la lune bleue nous faire partager l' même ombre,je suis parti en redemande.

Despite timeless lingerings, day fell to night.
Reality now coming to my consciousness.
We returned to the threshold this time transformed.
I entered his world as a friend,
but because the blue moon let us share the same shadow,
I left wanting more.

Comme la Chaleur Monte

Nombreux mois de lunes d'été des ombres sur nous.
Le temps accordé éclairagenous permettant de voir clairement l'autre.

L'horloge nous permet de progresser.Temps nous enseigne pas comme les autres.Révéler ce qui est destiné à être,à apprendre et à se rapprocher ensemble.

De nombreuses expériences partagées àl'ombre des lunes passionnés.Notre première nuit sur, dîner, vinavec de nombreuses soirées après.

Parties, les amis et les jours fériés apprécié ensemble.Notre premier baiser sous le gui,été autorisés à prolongerjusque dans les profondeurs de froid et la neige.

Le temps qui passe fleuri passion.Nous avons été attirés dans le désir. Je suis excité par sa seule présence.Il dit qu'il est fou, sauvage par mon sourire.

Amour continue à s'entrainer plus profondément, que la chaleur s'élève à des hauteurs érotiques. Ma prière est pour l'été de restergoûter la douceur de vivre.

As Heat Rises

Many months of Summer moons
cast shadows upon us.
The time granted illumination
allowing us to see each other clearly.

The clock moves us forward.
Time teaches us like no other.
Revealing what is destined to be,
to learn and grow closer together.

Many experiences shared under
the shadows of passionate moons.
Our first night out, dinner, wine
with many evenings after.

Parties, friends, and holidays enjoyed together.
Our first kiss under the mistletoe,
allowed Summer to extend
even in the depths of cold and snow.

Time passing bloomed passion.
We were drawn into desire.
I'm aroused simply by his presence.
He says he's crazed, wild by my smile.

Love continues to root deeper,
as heat rises to erotic heights.
My prayer is for Summer to remain
tasting the sweetness of life.

Solstice d'été

*Le soleil se réveille le ciel
est chuchotant sonnets aux jardins, mon âme.
Feuilles, les fleurs, mon coeur, notretronçon vœuxcorps,
ouvrant des rayons touchent.*

*Embrassant la chaleur, la passion de la journée la plus longue
de l'été. Réalité dépasse enfinles de mes rêves combinés.*

*Nous posons ainsi que deux pas, mais comme celui-ci.Sachant
indépendamment aligner nos âmesreliant à des
profondeursjamais connu.*

*La journée est longue, nous pouvons prendre notre temps
àapprendre et à découvrir que le soleil se déplace vers
l'ouest.Nous continuons à tomber plus profondémentavec sa
main maintenant tenir la mienne.*

Summer Solstice

The sun awakens the East sky
whispering sonnets to the gardens, my soul.
Leaves, blooms, my heart, our bodies stretch
greeting, opening from rays touching.

Embracing the heat, the passion
of the longest Summer's day.
Reality finally surpasses
all of my dreams combined.

We lay together not as two, but as one.
Knowing independently our souls align
connecting at depths
never before experienced.

The day is long, we can take our time
learning and discovering as the sun travels west.
We continue to fall more deeply
with his hand now holding mine.

La chaleur de soupir désir de la journée couvre une table sur la véranda du jardin. Un régal chaud préparé ensemblenous apporte la clarté, la sensibilisation et la grâce.

Notre table éclairée par des bougies de bois de santal et decèdre, les flammes amélioré le coucher de soleil rougeoyant. Les rosiers grimpants décorée colonnes de la véranda. Une musique douce mettre de l'essence.

Réflexion sur notre relation comme il versa le vin. Se souvenir de notre premier bonjouralors comment nos coeurs enlacés.

L'chandelles accentué la couleur de la passionque nous avons partagé bien dans nuit. l'Unitéa une signification nouvelle. Etre aimé cette profondeur, exaltante, et réconfortant.

Nous avons adopté notre cadeau de connexion complète tandis que nous avons cultivé l'amour le plus pur. Sur son genou avec une promesse et un baiserplacé un anneau symbolisant à jamais.

The heat of the day's longing sigh
covers a table on the garden's veranda.
A hot feast prepared together
brings us clarity, awareness, and grace.

Our table lit with sandalwood and cedar candles,
the flames enhanced the glowing sunset.
The climbing roses decorated the veranda's columns.
Soft music set the essence.

Reflecting on our relationship
as he poured the wine.
Remembering our first hello
then how our hearts entwined.

The candlelight heightened the flush of passion
as we shared well into the night.
Unity has new meaning.
Being loved this deeply, exhilarating, and comforting.

We embraced our gift of complete connection
while we cultivated the purest love.
On his knee with a promise and a kiss
placed a ring symbolizing forever.

Mariage d'été

Leméandres chemin que le tempset Dieu a ordonné est devenu plus droit.Ce qui autrefois était l'ombre, avec de grosses mauvaises herbesdenses est maintenant vert, croissant avec des graines abondantes.

Il a vu nos années de solitude.
Il a vu notre passé plein de désespoir.Il nous a guidés pour répondre àconnaître nos désirs et de peurs.

Mon véritable amour m'a amené à ce bel endroit, les années de confiance, cependant, jamais une course.Dans le temps d'aimer et nourrir grâce.Il a ouvert nos cœurs avec sa main aimante.

Maintenant, nous en sommes, ensemble, sur l'alléed'or bordéeavec des fleurs d'été brillants. lis, iris, roses, hortensias et nous bénir avec toutes leurs nuances et les parfums.

Le monde est maintenant plein de musique et le chantdes oiseaux et les anges se réjouissent. .Pour notre avenir, nous traitons chantant.

Summer Wedding

The meandering path which time
and God directed has become straighter.
What once was shadowed, with thick dense weeds
is now green, growing with abundant seeds.

He saw our years of loneliness.
He saw our past full of despair.
He guided us to meet
knowing our desires and fears.

My true love has brought me to this beautiful place,
years of trusting, though, never a race.
In time with loving and nurturing grace.
He opened our hearts with His loving hand.

Now we stand, together, on the golden aisle
lined with brilliant summer blooms.
Lilies, irises, roses, and hydrangeas
bless us with all of their shades and fragrances.

The world is now full of music and song
from the birds and angels rejoicing.
To our future, we process along
with all of us together, singing.

Autumn

Life is a process of becoming, a combination of states we have to go through. Where people fail is that they wish to elect a state and remain in it.
 This is a kind of death.

> ~ Anais Nin

Brises Fraîches de Conscience

*Au cœur de la chaleur estivale
une brise fraîche me glaça le dos
perçant mon cœur
des pensées refoulées me venant clairement a l'esprit.*

*Pendant des années, des étés, je l'ai vraiment aimé.
Les sentiments intenses que j'ai ressentis étaient partagés.
Le poids de la vie a comprimé nos cœurs,
Les passions ont fané dans la routine, mondaine.*

*Est-ce que je l'aime toujours?
Oui, mais j'ai dumal à répondre.
Est-ce qu'il m'aime toujours?
Sa réponse était oui d'une manière froide sans émotion.*

*Au fil du temps l'amour a changé
des liens profonds autrefois ressentis,
les chaînes de notre amour ont fondu
en silence et éloignement.*

*Conversations jadis partagées,
désormais les réponses sont réduites à un seul mot.
Le seul contact échangé,
des regards de colère au plus fort de nos disputes.*

Cool Breezes of Consciousness

In the midst of Summer's heat
a cool breeze chilled my spine
piercing my heart
bringing suppressed thoughts to clarity of mind.

For years of Summers, I truly loved him.
The intense feelings I felt were exchanged.
The weight of life has compressed our hearts,
passions fade into mundane, routine.

Do I still love him?
Yes, but I am struggling to answer.
Does he still love me?
His reply was yes in a cold emotionless manner.

Over time love has changed
from deep connections once felt,
our bonds of love have melted
to silence and avoidance.

Conversations once shared,
now answers are reduced to a single word.
The only eye contact exchanged,
looks of anger during the heat of battle.

Nous nous heurtons sur des sujets sans importance.
Mon esprit pleure alors que je sens mon âme partir.
Ses frustrations croissantes, explosives.
Mes prières muettes de protection, suppliant.

C'est devenu le mode de vie.
Vide de rire, bonheur et joie.
Dans mon jardin, je m'échappe
pour quelques moments volés de paix.

Est-ce ce que Dieu voulait?
Est-ce ce que le mariage signifie?
Est-ce sain pour les enfants?
Mais sur l'autel une promesse fut faite.

We collide over subjects with very little meaning.
My spirit tears while I feel my soul leave.
His growing frustrations, explosive.
My mental prayers of protection, pleading.

This has become the way of life
void of laughter, happiness, and joy.
In my garden, I escape
for stolen moments of peace.

Is this what God intended?
Is this what marriage means?
Is this healthy for the children?
But on the altar a promise made.

Chaleur Accablante.

L'air est stagnant d'humidité pesante.
Le soleil en fin d'après-midi, tape mortellement.
Sous la chaleur, trempée de sueur et de larmes d'incertitude.

Je me souviens de dizaines d'étés.
Ma force vitale innée diminue
avec chaque année qui passe.

Maintenant je suis assise plus âgée, épuisée, vide d'émotions,
inexpressive, et pourtant nostalgique de la passion ravivée
d'étés lointains.

Quelle saison vient à moi?

En ce jour accablant
je m'accroche à tout ce qui me reste
sur les genoux contre la clôture du jardin.

Priant pour un sursis,
des réponses, direction, et clarté des chemins.
Ensuite, une brise d'un froid intense m'a caressé la joue.

Mais l'odeur dans l'air, inattendue.

J'ai parcouru du regard le jardin en direction de l'horizon. Les
vents changent avec nuages gris sombres qui se forment.
Une tempête arrive.

Oppressive Heat.

The air is stagnant with humidity weighing.
The late afternoon sun, deadly beating.
The heat drenching me with sweat and tears of uncertainty.

I am remembering decades of Summers.
My innate life force declining
with each passing year.

Now I sit older, exhausted, void of emotion,
expressionless, yet yearning for a rekindled passion
of Summers from long ago.

What season is upon me?

On this oppressive day
I cling to all I have remaining
on my knees against the garden's fence.

Praying for a reprieve,
answers, direction, clarity of paths.
Then an intense cold breeze caressed my cheek.

But the smell in the air, unexpected.

I gazed across the garden looking toward the horizon.
The winds are changing with gray dark clouds forming.
A storm coming.

Equinoxe d'Automne

Nous avons été guidés il y a bien des années à ce sanctuaire.
Cœurs ouverts esprits enflammés musique envahissante.
Le Fils a révélé Sa volonté pour notre avenir,
avec des profondeurs infinies de possibilités.

Je savais quand tu étais disponible.
Je savais aussi quand tu étais distant.
La dichotomie sombre, la confusion ancrée à l'intérieur,
t'empêchaient d'être pleinement guidé.

Avons-nous jamais été
cœurs ouverts esprits enflammés musique envahissante?
Ou la vie est elle
une illusion masquant la réalité volant la lumière intérieure?

Lorsque tu t'écartas de mon étreinte,
retirant mes bras de ta taille,
le regard dans tes yeux, le stress sur ton visage,
je savais à ce moment-là, l'été était fini.

Autumnal Equinox

We were guided many years ago to this sanctuary.
Hearts opened spirits soaring music surrounding.
The Son revealed His will for our future,
with endless depths of possibilities.

I knew the times you were open.
I also knew the times you were distant.
The dark dichotomy, confusion imbedded within,
inhibited you to fully be led.

Were ever our
hearts opened spirits soaring music surrounding?
Or was life
illusions masking reality stealing light within?

When you stepped away from my embrace,
lowered my arms from around your waist,
the look in your eyes, the stress on your face,
I knew at that moment, summer ended.

La Grille du Jardin

*Il fut un temps au plus fort de l'été
où je regardais dans tes yeux, un miroir de Dieu lui-même.
Son sourire en coin, son rire exubérant,
la musique, son esprit, m'attiraient.*

*J'ai tenu bon, à genoux
priant Dieu de faire disparaître
les sentiments dont je savais
qu'ils n'auraient pas dû être.*

*Fermez cette porte je suppliais
tous les esprits qui voudraient bien écouter.
Ces prières sont restées sans réponse
Alors que les bougies allumées miroitaient.*

*C'est de moi, je vous ai mené ici,
était tout ce que je pouvais entendre.
Les pages du calendrier ont tourné et les choses ont évolué,
ou c'est ce qu'il me semblait.*

*Un clin d'œil, un sourire chaleureux à la suite d'un regard
amical,
un toucher doux, une étreinte aimante
comment cela pourrait marcher, je ne m'en souciais pas.*

The Garden Gate

There was a time during the height of Summer
when I gazed into his eyes, a mirror of God himself.
His crooked smile, his exuberant laugh,
the music, his spirit, sucked me in.

I stood my ground, on my knees
begging God to take away
the feelings that I knew
shouldn't be.

Close this door I begged
to all spirits who would listen.
These prayers were not answered
as the burning candles glistened.

This is from me, I led you here,
was all that I could ever hear.
Calendar pages turned and things progressed,
or that is what it seemed to me.

A wink, a warm smile following a friendly stare,
a soft touch, a caring embrace
how this could work,
I did not care.

*Alors que je pensais ressentir les profondeurs de l'amour,
en réalité pas lui.
Les sentiments changent, tout comme ces saisons
de choix qui sont faits, pour de nombreuses raisons.*

*Les vents changent en un instant.
L'air devient froid.
A un point crucial
d'un mot écrit, non.*

*J'ai senti Dieu me mener vers le chemin
du bonheur et de la joie, en regardant en arrière.
A la fin il n'y avait rien, qu'une grande
grille en fer forgé, verrouillée et noire.*

*Avec lui ai demandé la clé.
Il dit qu'il ne peut pas l'ouvrir,
un don de choix libre à toi.*

*Je suis restée à le regarder du mauvais côté de la grille son
m'énerve, dois-je attendre?
Je m'interroge sur mon passé, mon avenir incertain
mon travail, ma vision, mon a priori, nier.*

For I thought I felt the depths of love
in reality he did not.
Feelings change, just as these seasons
from choices made, for many reasons.

The winds change in an instant.
The air becomes cold.
At a pivotal point
with a written word, no.

I felt God was leading me down the garden path
toward happiness and joy, looking back.
At the end there was nothing but a tall
wrought iron gate, locked and black.

With Him standing next to me,
I asked him for the key.
He says He can not open it,
a gift of free will to thee.

I stood looking at him from the wrong side of the gate
his posteriori enrages me, should I wait?
I am questioning my past, uncertain of my future
my work, my vision, my a priori, negate.

Alors que les fleurs d'été mourraient,
les bulbes d'automne et les couleurs brillaient.
Je me tenais à la grille verrouillée
en train d'imploser, folle.

Tout ce que j'avais connu, ressenti, rêvé,
m'a poussé contre cette grille.
L'air froid d'automne a pris de la force.
Contre la grille je dois attendre

As the Summer blooms died
the fall bulbs and colours blazed.
I stood at the locked gate
imploding, crazed.

Everything I knew, felt, dreamt,
pushed me against this gate.
The cold fall air gains strength.
Against the gate, I must wait.

Automne

J'ai pleuré sous la lune des moissons
car aujourd'hui une saison est morte.

Le temps érode, les vents virent au froid,
les couleurs glorieuses palissent, et passent.

Pensées et sentiments doivent maintenant se rendre
Pour survivre aux mois solitaires et froids à venir.

Malgré l'attente d'une étreinte chaleureuse,

le soleil sur mon visage me manque.

Je me souviens des jardins verdoyants et en fleurs,
mais ce qui a poussé maintenant a une fin.

Autumn

I cried under the harvest moon
for today a season died.

Time erodes, the winds turn cold,
the glorious colours fade, and descend.

Thoughts and feelings now must turn in
to survive the lonely cold months ahead.

Despite longing for a warm embrace,
I miss the Sun touching my face.

I remember the lush green gardens and blooms
but that which was growing now has an end.

Winter

"That time of year thou mayst in me behold
When yellow leaves, or none, or few, do hang
Upon those boughs which shake against the cold,
Bare ruin'd choirs, where late the sweet birds sang.
In me thou seest the twilight of such day
As after sunset fadeth in the west,
Which by and by black night doth take away,
Death's second self, that seals up all in rest.
In me thou see'st the glowing of such fire
That on the ashes of his youth doth lie,
As the death-bed whereon it must expire
Consumed with that which it was nourish'd by.
This thou perceivest, which makes thy love more strong,
To love that well which thou must leave ere long."

~ William Shakespeare, *Shakespeare's Sonnets*

Mort en Vivant

Volontairement, avec mon cœur et l'âme ouverts,
j'avançais dans l'allée centrale.
Fleurs et parfums bordaient mon chemin,
de la musique jouait doucement au loin.

Dans ce sanctuaire, ici, j'ai été élevée.
Nous nous sommes agenouillés à l'autel.
Nous avons confessé nos péchés, échangé des anneaux,
communié.
Ensuite, j'ai promis devant Dieu, je lui soumettrais ma vie.

Petite fille c'est ce qu'on m'a appris à rêver.
J'ai été élevée dans mes beaux habits du dimanche.
Mon mari, ma famille, et mon église tenaient première place
dans ma vie et mes passions abandonnées.

J'ai servi quatre décennies
travaillant sans relâche.
J'ai suivi les instructions, les commandements et les demandes
laissant se faner mon âme et moi-même.

Death in Living

Willingly, with my heart and mind open,
I processed down the center aisle.
Flowers and fragrances lined my path,
music softly performed in the distance.

In this sanctuary, here, I was raised.
We knelt down on the altar.
We confessed our sins, exchanged rings, fed communion.
Then, I promised before God, I would submit my life to him.

As a young girl this is what I was taught to dream.
I was raised in my Sunday's best.
My husband, my family, and my church came first
with my life and my passions laid to rest.

I served four decades
working tirelessly.
I followed instructions, commandments, and demands
with a knowing my spirit and myself fading.

*Joyeusement, j'ai travaillé et j'ai prié
jusqu'à cette journée d'automne.
La sueur asservissante de l'oppression
bloquait toute lumière et pesait lourd.*

*Mes efforts toujours insuffisants, même avec les meilleures
intentions.
Donner le meilleur de moi n'était jamais assez.
Personne ne pourrait exceller ni se développer
sous ces demandes, lois et conditions.*

*La notion du moi perdue, mon sentiment d'importance parti
après toute une vie de croyances.
Mon mari et mon église suscitaient la puissance, le contrôle et
la conformité.
Est-ce là ce que Dieu souhaitait?,*

*Vivre la vie, à servir et obéir
passant machinalement toutes les traditions.
Chaque aspect de ma vie est "très bien"
tant que je ne doute pas.*

Joyfully, I worked and prayed
until one Autumn day.
The slaving sweat of oppression
blocked all light and weighed heavy.

My efforts always fell short, even with the best intentions.
My best was never good enough.
No one could excel and thrive
under these demands, laws, and conditions.

My sense of self lost, my sense of worth gone
through a lifetime of beliefs.
My husband and my church elicited power, control, and
conformity.
Is this what God intended?

Living life, serving, and obeying
going through the traditional motions.
Every aspect of my life is "just fine"
as long as I do not question.

*On me dit quand m'asseoir, me tenir debout, adorer, et
m'agenouiller.
Soumise à la conformité et au pouvoir
de plusieurs autorités,
mari, Dieu, pasteur, pape, et père.*

*Lorsque l'autorité décide quelque chose de nouveau,
ses besoins, visions et changements radicaux.
Je suis censée suivre complètement
Changeant mes règles et traditions.*

*Tant que ses besoins sont satisfaits et les traditions perpétuées.
Tant que je ne doute pas, n'exprime pas mes propres pensées et
désirs.
Tant qu'il veut encore de moi parce que je satisfais ses besoins.
Alors la vie continue d'avancer sans interruptions, comblée.*

*Si vous n'acceptez-pas les exigences du chef de maison,
y a-t'il une place à la table?
L'individualité n'est acceptée que pour une brève minute,
encore une fois, ne jamais remettre en question l'autorité.*

I am told when to sit, stand, worship, and kneel.
Submitting to conformity and power
to levels of authority
husband, God, pastor, pope, and father.

When the authority decides something new,
his wants, visions, and paradigm changes.
I am expected to follow completely
changing my rules and traditions.

As long as his needs are met and traditions carried.
As long as I do not question, express my own thoughts,
and desires.
As long as he still wants me because I fulfill his needs.
Then life steadily moves forward, happily.

If you do not conform to the demands of the head of the house,
is there a seat at the table?
Individuality is accepted only in a minute range,
again, authority never questioned.

Dans les confins de murs de pierres appelés maison,
Est-ce qu'il écoute même ou sait?
Mes sentiments, mes exploits et ma vie sont-ils exaltés?
Est-ce de l'amour ou d l'autorité?

Voici ce que la Bible dit
et la façon dont elle est interprétée.
Dieu a-t-il inventé ces règles?
Est-ce vraiment la manière dont Il veuille que je vive?

Dans chaque maison, les lois sont enseignées différemment.
Chaque maison suit ses propres règles.
L'oppression est-elle toujours la même?
Personne n'ose poser la question.

Parce que la vie est heureuse
si vous n'observez pas vraiment
la réalité
assis en face à la table et la chaire.

In the confining stone walls called home,
does he even listen or know?
Are my feelings, accomplishments, and life exalted?
Is this love or control?

This is what the Bible says
and how it is interpreted.
Did God make these rules?
Is this really how He wants me to live?

In each house the laws are taught differently.
Each house follows its own set of rules.
Is the oppression still the same?
No one dares to question.

Because life is happy
if you don't really look
at reality
sitting across the table and the pulpit.

*Si vous ne mettez pas en doute ni ne vous souciez
que vous n'êtes pas vraiment vivant.
Alors exister au sein de la fausse sécurité de ce pouvoir, facile.
Jusqu'à ce que vous n'arriviez pas à subvenir à ses besoins et
puis... quoi ?*

*Je suis accrochée à cette barrière noire et froide
de quatre décennies de croyances.
Je suis enterrée au fond la neige glacée.
Je ne peux pas voir mes pieds.*

*Parce que je n'ai pas résisté,
mon identité et mes passions perdues.
J'ai passé ma vie à servir
les lois gravées sur la croix.*

*Est-ce la perte de Dieu en qui j'avais fidèlement confiance?
Est-ce la perte d'esprit et de moi attendue?
Est-ce ce que j'adore et je crois?
Est-ce le poids de l'oppression ... Dieu ... l'amour?*

If you do not question or care
that you aren't really living.
Then existing within the false security of this power, easy.
Until you do not meet his needs and then… what?

I am clinging to this cold black fence
from four decades of beliefs.
I am buried in the deep frozen snow.
I cannot see my feet.

Because I have not stood on my own,
my identity and passions lost.
I spent my life serving
the laws etched on the cross.

Is this loss from God whom I faithfully trusted?
Is this loss of spirit and self expected?
Is this what I worship and believe?
Is this weight of oppression…God… love?

Celle qui doute de la vie

Quels sont mes sentiments sur la vie, la mort?

Lorsque les branches et les fleurs se fanent,

Que se passe-t-il?

Est-ce que mon âme continuera?

Est-ce que mon Père viendra pour moi?

Est-ce que je Le verrai, quand les forces de la vie s'estompent et l'âme disparait?

Mes craintes abondent de pensées sur la mort.

Une peur à laquelle je ne peux faire face.

Comment la mort est-elle ressentie?

She Who Questions Life

What are my feelings of life, death?

When the branches and blooms fade,

what does happen?

Will my spirit move on?

Will my Father come for me?

Will I see Him, when life force fades and spirit leaves?

My fears abound the thought of death.

A fear I can not face.

How does death feel?

Attendre en Hiver

*Pendant ce temps gris et froid,
complètement gelé, toute énergie disparue.*

*La dernière force de vie qui reste
est la lumière la plus pâle.*

Je crois que même cela faiblit.

*La chaleur viendra-t-elle jamais?
Pourrais-je la ressentir à nouveau?*

*Où est la main de Dieu, l'étreinte du Fils?
Où est la musique, les anges, la grâce ?*

*L'espoir est-il encore là? Mon doute s'insinue.
La lumière devient faible.*

*Se souvenir, attendre le soleil,
Le printemps reviendra-t-il?*

Alors, je continue à attendre dans l'obscurité.

Waiting in Winter

During this cold grey time,
completely frozen, energy gone.

The only life force left
is but the dimmest light.

I even believe that will fade.

Will warmth ever come?
Will I ever feel again?

Where is God's hand, the Son's embrace?
Where is the music, the angels, the grace?

Is hope still within? My doubt creeps in.
The light is getting dim.

Remembering, longing for the Sun,
Will Spring ever come?

So, I continue to wait in darkness.

Solstice d'hiver

Le Temps a reculé, la nuit est si longue.
Le soleil va-t-il se lever?

Obscurité, des heures avant le matin
réveillée, derrière ka porte, des sons étranges de calme,
froid, encore une fois, seule.

Fermant les yeux, pensées emballées sous l'inquiétude,
Seulement par habitude, le cœur battant
certainement pas de passion ou d'amour
ni même sans fin.

Une âme infidèle, incapable de bouger, figée
se souciant du soleil qui ne se lève pas
puis qu'il se lève enfin.

Un esprit terni par la peur
la solitude toujours si évidente
pendant ce temps, la nuit la plus longue de l'année.

Winter Solstice

Time has fallen back, the night is so long.
Will the sunrise come?

Darkness, hours before morning
awoken, outside the gate, to eerie sounds of quiet,
cold, again, alone.

Eyes closing, mind anxiously racing,
only from habit, heart beating,
certainly not from passion or love
or even purpose.

A faithless soul, unable to move, frozen
worrying about the sun not rising
then worrying that it will.

A spirit tarnished with fear
loneliness has made ever so clear
during this, the longest night of the year.

Jour du Carême

*En ces temps obscures et solitaires
Sa présence me manque.*

*Où êtes-vous?
Existez-vous vraiment?*

*Ensuite, une voix résonne dans mon âme.
Je vous vois. Je suis juste hors de votre portée.*

*Je meurs contre cette porte. Je n'ai plus rien.
Si vous me voyez, alors pourquoi ne m'aidez-vous pas? Je crie.
Je vous protège. Je continue toujours à guider et à enseigner,
tout en vous permettant de venir me chercher dans les endroits
les plus sombres.*

*C'est terrifiant, j'ai crié dans la prière.
Que vais-je trouver d'inconnu?*

*Puis-je faire face à l'obscurité profonde
de ce mon âme contient?*

Lenten Journey

In this dark, lonely time
I'm longing for His presence.

Where are you?
Do you even exist?

Then, a voice resonating in my soul.
I do see you. I am just outside of your reach.

I'm dying against this gate. I have nothing left.
If you see me, then why don't you help me? I scream.
I am protecting you. I am still guiding and still teaching,
while allowing you to search for me in the darkest places.

This is terrifying, I cried out in prayer.
What unknowns will I find?

Can I face the deep darkness
of what my soul holds?

*Puis, j'entends. Souvenez-vous je suis partout, même à
l'intérieur.
Je ne suis pas confiné aux murs de pierres froides façonnés par
le pouvoir par l'homme.*

*Ce voyage vous est nécessaire pour explorer
et conquérir, cette obscurité que vous craignez.*

*Votre récompense sera grande à atteindre
force, paix , joie et vie pour commencer, encore une fois.*

Then, I hear. Remember I am everywhere even within.
I am not confined to the cold stone walls of manmade power.

This journey is necessary for you to explore
and conquer, this darkness in which you fear.

Your rewards will be great to win,
strength, peace, joy, and life to begin, again.

Attente du Printemps

*Dans la tranquillité, je suis au repos
sous un manteau blanc de protection
contre le monde froid et amer de chaos et de désespoir.*

*Attendant la fin de la saison de la solitude,
je me détends, me repose dans le confort
car le Soleil sait que je suis ici.*

*Sous ce manteau, j'attends
même si j'attends avec détermination
le temps n'est pas perdu.*

*Pour l'instant, ma force se développe,
mes racines s'approfondissent,
attendant avec le Soleil.*

Waiting on Spring

In the stillness, I am dormant
under a white blanket of protection
from the cold bitter world of chaos and despair.

Waiting for the season of loneliness to end,
I relax, rest, in comfort,
for the Sun knows I am here.

Under this blanket, I wait
though I wait with purpose
time not wasted.

For now, my strength grows,
my roots deepen,
waiting with the Sun.

Spring

And the day came when the risk it took
to remain tight inside the bud was more painful
than the risk it took to blossom.

~ Anais Nin

La Fonte de Neige

J'ai toujours, froid, sans vie, immobile
sous une bâche d'hibernation
doutant d'une aube nouvelle.

Ensuite, le Soleil vient,
La lumière du jour réchauffe la Terre.
La neige se transforme en nourriture
cherchant mes racines.

Respirant profondément, je m'étire,
bougeant, me détendant avec chaque respiration.
Les frémissements de vie, je les sens
me traverser à chaque inspiration.

Je redécouvre la vie, réchauffant mon âme.
Mes racines s'enfoncent, les feuilles commencent à grandir.
Pousser vers le ciel.
Mon passé a fondu, l'hiver a survécu.

The Melting of Snow

I'm still, cold, lifeless, motionless
under a tarp of hibernation
doubting a new dawn.

Then, the Sun comes,
daylight warms the Earth.
Snow turns to nourishment
seeking my roots.

Breathing deeply, I stretch,
moving, unwinding with each breath.
The pulse of life, I feel
running through me with each inhale.

I rediscover life, warming my soul.
My roots deepen, leaves begin to grow.
Pushing up toward the sky.
My past melted, winter survived.

Renaitre

*Regardant à travers le jardin,
une fontaine de pierres à trois niveaux apparu.
J'ai tourné le dos à la barrière,
et marché pour m'en approcher.*

*L'eau dans la fontaine
contenait le présent que j'attendais de découvrir.
J'ai senti la guérison m'envahir,
puis j'ai submergé mes mains plus profondément.*

*Les reliques de l'automne et de l'hiver,
les larmes séchées sur mes joues,
je joins mes mains, agenouillée,
pour me laver le visage et les pieds.*

*L'eau a non seulement enlevé la saleté,
la purification est allée beaucoup plus loin,
la guérison a trouvé son chemin vers chaque cellule
de mes yeux, mon cœur, mon âme et mon esprit.*

*Cette guérison complète a pris juste un instant,
avec les pouvoirs divins de l'eau qui coule.
Toutes choses peuvent être lavées et purifiées
et changées à jamais éternellement.*

Rebirth

Gazing across the garden,
a three tiered stone fountain appeared.
I turned my back upon the gate,
and walked, to bring it near.

The water in the fountain
contained the gift I longed to experience.
I felt the healing come through me,
then submerged my hands more deeply.

The residue from Autumn and Winter,
the crusted tears upon my cheeks,
I cupped my hands, kneeling down,
to wash my face and feet.

The water not only removed the dirt,
the cleansing went much deeper,
the healing found its way to each cell
in my eyes, heart, soul, and spirit.

This complete healing took just an instant,
in the Divine powers of flowing water.
All things can be washed and cleansed
and changed eternally forever.

Maintenant je me tiens debout, je m'étire, et respire,
accueillant l'air du printemps dans mes poumons.
Sentant l'herbe verte fraîche sous mes pieds,
avec la chaleur du soleil descendant en cascade.

C'est le temps des renouveaux,
Le printemps est là, enfin
les enfants chantent, les oiseaux gazouillent,
la vie à nouveau, épanouie.

Now I stand, stretch, inhale,
inviting Spring air into my lungs.
Feeling fresh green grass beneath my feet,
with the warmth of the Sun cascading down.

It is a time of new beginnings,
Spring is here, at last
children singing, birds chirping,
life again, blooming.

Jour de Mai

A genoux contre la fontaine en pierres,
c'est une guérison complète, que j'ai reçue.
Le passé a été lavé, purifié,
une nouvelle vie, pour moi, débutera aujourd'hui.

Larmes de joie viennent exploser.
De mes yeux, une rivière qui coule.
Tout ce qui avait besoin de s'échapper
jaillit immédiatement en ruisselant.

Après les pouvoirs de l'eau
je me suis effondrée prostrée sur le sol,
recueillant l'énergie de la Terre
absorbant le don de guérison.

Après ce qui me parut plusieurs années,
mais fut, en réalité, seulement quelques minutes,
mes yeux se sont ouverts d'un regard clair
me sentant jeune, en bonne santé, avec un objectif.

Ma vie, aujourd'hui, a été transformée,
le Soleil m'a donné un cadeau.
Le passé, de nombreuses saisons,
évaporé, fini, à la dérive.

May Day

Kneeling against the stone fountain,
a complete healing, I received.
The past has been washed clean,
a new life, for me, will begin today.

Tears of joy came exploding.
From my eyes, a river flowing.
Everything needing releasing
came instantly streaming.

From the power of the water
I collapsed prostrate on the ground,
collecting energy from the Earth
absorbing healing coming down.

After what seemed like years
though, actually, only minutes,
my eyes opened with clear new sight
feeling young, healthy, with a vision.

Life for me, today, was transformed,
the Sun gave me a gift.
The past, of many seasons,
evaporated, finished, adrift.

Mon avenir m'appartient,
je sais qu'il sera bon
mené par Dieu, son Fils, et les anges.
Sans fardeau, ni retenue.

Les possibilités, illimitées,
paix, joie, bonheur de consommer.
Mes pensées avant-gardistes de passions
une ardoise vierge, privilégiée, la vie de nouveau.

My future is up to me
I know good is coming
with God, Son, and angels leading.
without the weight, holding.

The possibilities, limitless
peace, joy, happiness consume.
My forward thoughts of passions
a blank slate, entitled, Life Anew,

Le Portail se Réchauffe

*Le soleil brille Ses rayons
éclairant le jardin autour de moi.
Même le portail ne semble pas aussi noir
aussi froid ni aussi menaçant.*

*Assise au même endroit
où j'étais pendant l'automne et l'hiver.
Sombre, petit, terrifiant, et suffocant,
à présent, aujourd'hui, c'est très différent.*

*Pour l'instant, je vois la beauté de mon côté du portail,
Des magnolias avec de douces fleurs roses, alignés en bordure
du jardin.
Tulipes, jonquilles, lys se tiennent debout sous l'arbre.
Crocus violets, jaunes, blancs surgissent dessous.*

*Je me retourne et regarde entre les larges barres de fer forgé
noir.
L'Esprit a levé le voile qui pendant des décennies aveuglait.
La lumière du soleil illumine mes bénédictions, mes leçons,
et le chemin que je devrais suivre désormais.*

The Gate Turns Warm

The Sun shines His rays
enlightening the garden around me.
Even the gate does not seem as black
as cold and as threatening.

I sit in the middle of this same space
I did during Autumn and Winter.
Dark, small, terrifying, and suffocating,
now, today, it's much different.

For now, I see the beauty of my side of the gate.
Magnolia trees, with soft pink blooms, line the garden's edge.
Tulips, daffodils, lilies stand tall under the tree.
Purple, yellow, white crocuses pop up beneath.

I turn and look between the thick black wrought iron bars.
The Spirit lifted the veil which for decades was blinding.
Sunlight illuminated my blessings, my lessons,
and my path I now should take.

Construire la porte était son choix,
son libre arbitre et sa décision,
avec de nouveaux désirs, de nouvelles passions, il avait besoin
de diriger son chemin dans une nouvelle direction.

Maintenant, il dit qu'il est heureux
son jardin est à son goût
Quoi que, je ne vois pas sa joie,
sa décision n'est pas la mienne.

Je peux maintenant toucher ce portail
car il n'est plus noir, froid ni menaçant.
Avec une nouvelle clarté, j'en vois la valeur
maintenant c'est un symbole de force.

To build the gate was his choice
his free will and his decision,
with new desires, new passions, he needed to
steer his path in a different direction.

Now, he says he is happy;
his garden does suit his taste.
Although, I do not see his joy,
his decision is not my place.

I am now able to touch this gate
for it is no longer black, cold, and threatening.
With new found clarity I see the blessing
now it is a symbol of strength.

Transformation

*Je suis retournée à un endroit qui fut un temps ma résidence
après bien de nombreuses années.
Ce que j'ai trouvé je n'avais pas prévu,
il y a eu peu de changements.*

*Est-ce que le temps s'arrête immobile encore dans cette ville
rurale?
J'ai été témoin de la preuve du temps qui passe,
le lever du soleil, le coucher de soleil
les étoiles dans leur ordre établi.*

Où est le changement?

*Le kiosque à musique est toujours debout fier et illuminé
au milieu du parc
sous les sons du groupe local
jouant la marche familière.*

Le changement n'est pas là.

Transformation

I returned to a place I once called home
after many years away.
What I found I did not foresee,
there were no changes to be.

Does time stand still in this rural town?
I witnessed evidence of time passing,
the sunrise, sunset
the stars in their proper arrangement.

Where is the change?

The bandshell still stands with lighted pride
in the middle of the park
with sounds from the community band
playing the familiar march.

Change is not there.

*L'épouse du clarinettiste avec son chapeau à larges bords
tricote encore pendant les chansons.
La journaliste de la ville griffonne ses notes, prend des photos
pendant qu'elle déambule.*

Le changement n'est pas là.

*Ah, l'odeur familière des côtelettes de porc grésillant sur le gril,
l'arôme emplit l'air.
Les dames de l'église luthérienne ont préparé des rangées de
tartes à partager
Laquelle vais-je prendre, peu m'importe.*

*Je suis heureuse le changement n'a pas pris place là-bas.
Je sais que le changement a lieu quelque part.*

*Les enfants grimpent toujours sur les portiques
se balançant sur les balançoires.
Plus haut, plus haut, ils crient et supplient
en riant.*

Seulement quelques mesures de changement ont eu lieu là.

Où est le changement, que je suis venue chercher?

The clarinetist's wife with her large brimmed hat
still knits throughout the songs.
The town's reporter scribbling notes, snapping pictures
as she walks along.

Change is not there.

Ah, the familiar scent of pork chops sizzling on the grill,
the aroma fills the air.
The ladies from the Lutheran church baked rows of pies to share
which one I take, I do not care.

I am glad change was not found there.
I do know change is somewhere.

The children are still climbing on the monkey bars
swinging on the swings.
Higher, Higher they laughingly scream
and plead.

Only a few inches of change was found there.

Where is the change, I came to find?

*Alors que la dernière côtelette de porc et dernière tarte
disparaissent
pendant que le groupe joue son dernier morceau
j'ai découvert où le changement était clé
c'était en moi tout au long.*

As the last pork chop and pie consumed
while the band played the last tune
I discovered where change was key
it was all along within me.

Réflexions
Mon cœur a été réchauffé par les rayons de lumière et nettoyés par l'eau ruisselante.
Cette force guérissante de voyager et de libérer les traces du passé,
pour garantir que mon avenir peut s'épanouir sans épines ni resté enfermé sous la crainte.

Pendant bien des saisons j'ai cherché la clé.
Elle était enfouie profondément dans la neige derrière la clôture.
Au-delà des blocs de barres de fer une ouverture qui était obscurcie par les ténèbres.

Enfin, j'ai choisi de voir l'ouverture et comment le soleil peut illuminer une nouvelle voie.
Mes choix et intentions m'ont permis de grandir, me transformer et être menée,
vers un chemin plein d'amour avec des possibilités nouvelles et passionnantes.

Aussi sûre que la lune qui tombe et le soleil se lève
comptant mon âge et mes expériences vers le sommet de ma vie.
Maintenant, je vois chaque décennie, chaque saison offerte
en cadeau, Cultures Saisonnières.

Reflections

My heart was warmed by rays of light
and cleansed by flowing water.
This healing gifted strength to travel
and release past footsteps,
to insure my future can blossom without thorns
nor locked behind fear.

Four many seasons I searched for the key.
It was deeply buried within the snow behind the fence.
Beyond the blocks of iron bars an opening that was obscured by darkness.

Finally, I chose to see the opening and how the
Sun can illume a new path.
My choices and intent allowed me to grow, transform,
and be led, to a path full of love with new and exciting possibilities.

As constant as the falling moon and the rising Sun
counting my age and experience towards the apex of my life.
Now I see each decade, each season as a gift, *Quartered Enlightenment.*

A note afterword
by Poet Sandra Marchetti   April 2013

A Fruitful Return: Reflections on Quartered Enlightenment

The poet Mary Ruefle, paraphrasing Paul Valéry, says, "The opening line of a poem is like finding...a piece of fallen fruit you have never seen before, and the poet's task is to create the tree from which such a fruit would fall." Trisha Georgiou's *Quartered Enlightenment* accomplishes this incredibly difficult undertaking. From the title we know that a transformation has occurred. The chapbook itself tells us the story of that enlightenment through prayers, encounters with the natural world, and a chorus of voices.

  Trisha's work functions as a chapbook in the truest sense of the word. Chapbooks began as religious tracts and commonplace books of prayers. As they were inexpensive to produce, these short works also promoted literacy and language learning. *Quartered Enlightenment* contains prayers that remind me of Rilke's pleadings in his *Book of Hours*. I hear him in poems like, "Oppresive Heat.": "On this oppressive day / I cling to all I have remaining / on my knees against the garden's fence." A vivid exploration of language is also present in the sonorous French translations. The sonic pleasure of reading the last stanza of "Marriage d'été" aloud is unparalleled.

    The poems speak most vibrantly when the natural world and human life are brought into balance. These spheres come into alignment at the beginning of the very first poem: "Plants blooming colorful and green. / They welcome me returning from worship, / waiting to accompany me." This sensibility of worship in the garden sets the tone for the work. I think of Emily Dickinson's poem that reads:

    Some keep the Sabbath going to Church

    I keep it staying at Home—

    With a Bobolink for a Chorister—

    And an Orchard, for a Dome—

The influence of Dickinson appears throughout the book; poetry and plant life are melded in lines like, "The sun awakens the East sky / whispering sonnets to the gardens, my soul" in "Summer Solstice."

Louise Glück's voice also echoes through Georgiou's work. I am reminded of Glück's seminal work, *The Wild Iris*, in the organization of *Quartered Enlightenment* around vespers, gardening, and domestic life. The poem, "Sharing the Shadow of the Moon," and its lines, "His charm led me further, / by lifting the weight from my shoulders, / taking my purse and the bag of fresh offerings" speak to Glück's early poem, "The Encounter": "I drew the gown over my head; / a red flush covered my face and shoulders. / It will run its course, the course of fire." Like in Glück's work, there is a danger in the poems of *Quartered Enlightenment*. An impending darkness shows itself in the final stanza of "Autumnal Equinox":

When you stepped away from my embrace,
lowered my arms from around your waist,

the look in your eyes, the stress on your face,

I knew at that moment, summer ended.

The author lets us know that the natural world affects humans as we affect it. Enlightenment, or spring, is an organic process that does not occur on our timetable. As the speaker marks a life, independence hatches. Winter is not a season of death; it is portrayed as necessary dormancy in "The Melting of Snow," "My roots deepen, leaves begin to grow. / Pushing up toward the sky. / My past melted, winter survived." Later in the text, we wait "*with* the sun" instead of "for it." Humans are an integral part of this landscape.

Quartered Enlightenment embodies native cycles. The poems respond to our historical moment regarding the cycles of marriage and divorce, climate change, and spirituality. At the same time, the book leads me back to the ancient rhythms of call and response, our dependence on nature, and interior and exterior life. Trisha Georgiou's poems tell us that the threat of disaster is continuously linked to the threat of untamed beauty, that wild burgeoning force. Georgiou impels us to confront these truths, head on. The growth that stems from this can be a terrifying process, but one with a tremendous yield. As the poet Dave Smith says, "no threat, no poem."

Sandra Marchetti *teaches writing and literature outside of her native Chicago. She completed her MFA in Creative Writing–Poetry at George Mason University in 2010. Sandra was named the winner of the Midwest Writing Center's 2011 Mississippi Valley Chapbook Contest for her volume,* The Canopy. *She was also a finalist in* Gulf Coast's *2011 Poetry Prize and her poems and reviews have appeared, or are forthcoming, in Ohio State's* The Journal, Nashville Review, Gargoyle, The Bakery, *and* Subtropics, *among others. She is currently the Poetry Editor of* Minerva Rising, *a journal of women and their stories, and she attended the 2012 Sewanee Writers' Conference. You can find her at sandrapoetry.net.*

A note ...

a thought....

a reflection...

toward your enlightenment.

About the Author

The essence of Quartered Enlightenment began nearly a decade ago in Trisha's garden. While tending to her roses Trisha contemplated how the plants felt living through each season.

This book originally began as a collection of poems about the plants in her Shakespeare garden. From this starting point Quartered Enlightenment evolved to the story it is today.

Trisha's interest in gardening and the arts began in early childhood. These passions have remained and find their way onto the pages of her literary endeavours.

Her works focus on gardening, horticultural therapy, alternative healing, and poetry. They have been printed in regional, national and international publications.

Trisha's first book of poetry, *My Name is A, Meeting the Letters of the Alphabet,* was published in 1999. Her mission with *My Name Is A* was to expose children to poetry while promoting learning and literacy. Trisha is a contributing author for Creative Writing Primer from The Midwest Writing Center.

She is also a volunteer and member of the Board of Directors for the Midwest Writing Center.

For more information, we invite you to visit our websites.
www.TrishaGeorgiou.com
www.PoolboyPublishing.com
www.MidwestWritingCenter.org